Contents

Words in **bold**
are explained on
pages 30 and 31.

What is autumn?

Autumn is the season after summer. The weather is growing cold and the days get shorter. It rains often and it can be very windy. Leaves turn red and brown and fall off the trees.

But even though autumn is cold, it can be lots of fun. You can play in the crunchy dead leaves, dress up for **Halloween**, and look forward to winter holidays.

The wind blows fallen leaves into crunchy piles.

Cats and dogs grow longer fur in autumn to help them keep warm.

In autumn, people, animals and plants get ready for the winter. Bees, butterflies and other insects stop flying around.

Flowers lose their petals, and their seeds fall to the ground.

Seasons

AUTUMN

Belitha Press

Anna Claybourne • Pictures by Stephen Lewis

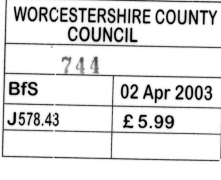

First published in the UK in 2001 by
Belitha Press
A member of Chrysalis Books plc
64 Brewery Road, London N7 9NT

Paperback edition first published in 2003
Copyright © Belitha Press Limited 2001
Text by Anna Claybourne

ISBN 1 84138 322 8 (hb)
ISBN 1 84138 747 9 (pb)

British Library Cataloguing in Publication Data
for this book is available from the British Library.

Printed in Hong Kong

10 9 8 7 6 5 4 3 2 1 (hb)
10 9 8 7 6 5 4 3 2 1 (pb)

Editor: Veronica Ross
Designer: Kathryn Caulfield
Illustrator: Stephen Lewis
Picture researcher: Juliet Duff
Consultant: Elizabeth Atkinson

Picture credits
Ancient Art and Architecture Collection: 22 R. Sheridan.
Bubbles: 18 Francs Rombout; 25 botttom Ian West.
FLPA: 7, 12 Mark Newman; 11 L. West; 13 A. Wharton;
25 top Terry Whittaker.
Getty One Stone: 4 Stewart Cohen; 5 Jane Gifford; 9 David Hisler;
10 top Alan Hicks; 10 bottom Jeremy Walker; 15 top Laurie Campbell;
16 Mitch Kezar; 19 Bruce Ayres; 20 Pauline Cutler.
NHPA: 14 Kevin Schafer; 15 bottom Dr Eckhart Pott;
17 E A Janes; 28 left BB Casals; 28 right Dick Jones.
Photofusion: 21 David Tothill.

Spring

Summer

Autumn

Winter

Autumn is one of the four seasons: spring, summer, autumn, and winter. Together the four seasons make up a year.

People wear warm clothes and put the heating on.

autumn fact

A big tree can drop 300 000 leaves every autumn.

The leaves on these lime trees are starting to turn yellow.

How autumn happens

The seasons are very different from each other. But do you know why they happen?

The Earth travels around the Sun once every year. The seasons happen because the Earth is tilted to one side. The tilt doesn't change. But as the Earth moves round the Sun in a big circle, the tilt makes different parts of the Earth point towards the Sun at different times.

These pictures show the seasons in the northern half of the world.

When your part of the world is tilted towards the Sun, the days are long and sunny. This is summer!

Autumn happens when the Earth begins to lean away from the Sun, and the weather becomes colder.

Spring

Spring happens in between winter and summer.

Sun

Autumn happens in between summer and winter.

Summer

Autumn

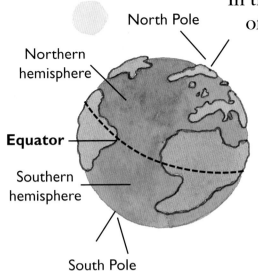

North Pole

Northern hemisphere

Equator

Southern hemisphere

South Pole

In the **northern hemisphere**, or northern half of the Earth, it is summer when the **North Pole** is tilted towards the Sun. It is winter when the North Pole is tilted away from the Sun. In the **southern hemisphere**, it is summer when the **South Pole** is tilted towards the Sun.

In winter, your part of the world is tilted away from the Sun.

Winter

Trees in North America are famous for their beautiful autumn colours.

autumn fact

In autumn, the days become shorter as we move away from the Sun.

Around the world

If you live in the northern hemisphere, autumn comes at the end of the year. So, if you live in Europe, America, China or Japan you will have autumn in September, October and November.

North Pole

Equator

South Pole

People who live on the equator don't have an autumn. For them it's hot all year round.

If you live in the southern hemisphere, autumn starts in March and lasts until May. So, for people in Australia, South Africa and Argentina, Easter is in the autumn.

Oysters are shellfish. They can be eaten raw or cooked.

autumn fact

In Ireland, autumn is the season for collecting oysters.

8

In autumn it is a **tradition** for people in China and Korea to go moongazing. The eighth full moon of the year is called the **Harvest Moon**, and it usually comes in September.

Everyone goes out to look at the moon. Then they eat special moon-shaped cakes.

In Mexico, 2 November is the Day of the Dead. Although this is a day for remembering dead people, it's not sad! There are feasts and fireworks, and bakers make skeleton-shaped sweets and bread.

These people are carrying models of skeletons made to celebrate the Day of the Dead.

Autumn weather

Autumn weather can change quickly. Some days are wet and windy, others are cold, bright and frosty.

On rainy autumn evenings, streetlights and car headlights reflect on to the shiny wet roads and pavements.

autumn fact

Smog is just what it sounds like – a mixture of smoke and fog.

Driving in **fog** can be very dangerous, so drivers must go slowly. Fog happens when the ground is freezing cold. This makes tiny drops of water in the air join together to make a big cloud on the ground.

Autumn winds blow leaves everywhere. Strong winds can blow tiles off rooftops and blow your umbrella inside out.

But sometimes, after autumn has started, there are a few days of warm, sunny weather. This is called an **Indian summer**.

Frost happens when drops of **dew** on grass and trees are frozen in cold weather. The sun shines on the frost and makes it sparkle.

Frost can form on windows too.

Plants in autumn

In autumn, leaves turn brown, dry and crinkly, and finally fall to the ground.

Trees lose water through their leaves. In winter, when the ground is frozen, it is hard for trees to take in water from the soil. So in autumn, trees shed their leaves. This makes the trees less thirsty and helps them stay alive in winter.

In summer, water escapes from trees' leaves.

In autumn, trees start losing their leaves.

Evergreens, such as fir trees and pine trees, often grow on mountainsides.

The leaves drop off one by one.

autumn fact
Evergreen trees stay green during the autumn, because they have spiny **needles** instead of leaves.

Sycamore trees grow wing-shaped seeds that spin around as the wind blows them through the air.

The seeds fall into the soil and wait there until the spring, when they will start to grow.

Some people say it is good luck to catch a falling leaf before it touches the ground.

Flowers wither away and make fruits and seeds.

Roses have fat, red **rose hips**, with lots of seeds inside.

You can see the remains of a **withered** flower on top of each rose hip.

Animals in autumn

Animals spend the autumn getting ready for winter. They have to find a way to stay alive when it is cold and there isn't much food around.

Bats, **marmots** and hedgehogs **hibernate**, or sleep through the winter. In the autumn, they eat lots of food until they are very fat, so they don't need to eat again until spring. Then they find a place to snuggle up and go to sleep.

Ladybirds cluster together to hibernate under dead leaves or in garden sheds.

These ladybirds are hibernating on a horsetail plant.

Bats hibernate together in a big bunch, hanging on to the ceiling of a cave or a cellar.

Squirrels and **pikas** spend the autumn collecting a big store of food to live on in the winter.

Snow geese, and many other birds, don't like the winter at all. Every autumn they travel, or **migrate**, from cold countries to warmer ones. They stay there until the spring comes.

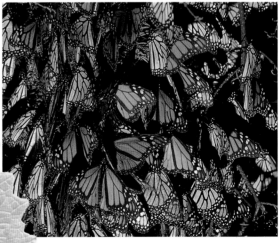

autumn fact

Monarch butterflies migrate 4000 km from North America to Mexico every autumn.

When they arrive in Mexico, monarch butterflies gather in big groups.

On the farm

Autumn is **harvest** time on the farm. The crops that were planted in the spring are now ready to collect.

Farmers use a big **combine harvester** to collect wheat. It cuts the stalks, shakes the grains of wheat off them, and collects the grains in a huge tank. The leftover stalks are thrown out of the back of the harvester as it drives along.

autumn fact

A combine harvester can cut 1000 wheat stalks every minute.

Potato farmers dig up the potatoes that have grown under the ground.

Most cows have their **calves** in autumn. It's hard work helping the babies to be born, and looking after them when they're little.

By the middle of autumn, apples are ripe and ready to pick. Farmers hire extra workers to pick the apples. But at some apple orchards, you can pick your own apples.

People in autumn

People get ready for autumn, just like animals. You might buy a new coat, an umbrella, or some waterproof wellies for splashing in puddles.

Gardeners sweep up fallen leaves. Some plants have to be covered to keep them warm.

autumn fact

When the days become shorter in autumn, the time is moved back one hour. This is so that we can have extra daylight in the mornings.

In autumn, it is time to go back to school after the long summer holidays. You might even be going to a new school, and meeting new friends.

You can help hungry birds by putting out nuts, seeds and bacon rind.

It's time to put away summer toys, sandpits, paddling pools and garden chairs.

Autumn festivals

Autumn can be cold and gloomy, but there are parties and **festivals** to cheer everyone up!

At a harvest festival, people give thanks for the crops that have been gathered that will see them through the winter.

Churches are decorated with flowers, fruit and vegetables, and food is collected to give away.

In Britain, there's an autumn festival on 5 November, called Bonfire Night. There are big bonfires and fireworks, and people eat special Bonfire Night food such as toffee and gingerbread.

autumn fact

Chinese people hold a kite-flying festival every autumn, on the ninth day of the ninth month.

Diwali, the **Hindu** festival of lights, takes place in October or November. People decorate their houses with rows of lamps to mark the arrival of winter, and there are bonfires and fireworks. Everyone prays to the **goddess** Lakshmi for a good year ahead.

Halloween, on 31 October, is the night when people used to believe that ghosts, witches and monsters came to haunt them.

Today, children wear all kinds of fancy dress costumes at Halloween. People decorate their houses with **lanterns** carved from **pumpkins**.

Autumn long ago

Long ago, there were no supermarkets, and hardly any food came from faraway countries. Most people ate food from local farms, or from their gardens.

After the harvest, people **preserved** food to stop it from going bad. Then they stored it for the winter – just like squirrels do! They made fruit into jam. Meat was smoked or salted to make it last longer.

In France, 500 years ago, people used to tread on the grapes they had harvested, to squash out the juice.

autumn fact

Bacon is a preserved meat that we still eat today.

The **Romans** had a harvest festival called **Pomona**. It was held to worship the goddess of trees and fruit. At the Pomona celebrations, there was a feast of apples, grapes and nuts.

22

The American festival of Thanksgiving began in 1621, when the first English settlers arrived in America. They had a hard, cold year, but their harvest was good, so they held a feast to celebrate.

Americans still remember this feast every November with a special Thanksgiving dinner of roast turkey and pumpkin pie.

Autumn dangers

In autumn, strong winds can blow branches off trees. Heavy rain makes roads and pavements slippery, so take care when you're out walking.

It's hard for drivers to see you in the dark. Be very careful when you cross the road.

autumn fact

Wasps leave their nests in the autumn, and sometimes come into houses. Keep away from them. A cold, grumpy wasp might sting you!

At the seaside, the wind whips up giant waves that crash on to the shore. They can smash houses or sweep people into the sea.

Reflective gear makes you glow in the dark!

If you ride a bike, it's a good idea to wear bright colours to make you easy to see at night.

Autumn activities

Here are some fun activities
to try this autumn.

Bright lights at night

Here's how to make a picture
of a dark, foggy night.

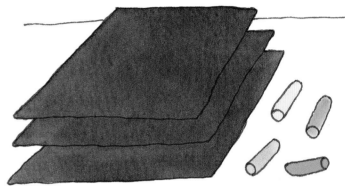

You need black, dark grey or dark
blue paper, and chalks or pastels.

Use yellow and white chalks to draw
lit-up windows, car headlights, or the
lights on a plane or spaceship.

To make a light look as if it's
glowing, gently smudge it round
and round with your finger.

Leaf pictures

If you collect some clean, dry fallen leaves, you can use them to make leaf pictures.

Glue the leaves to paper to make a leafy autumn **collage**.

Brush some wet paint over the back of a leaf, then press it on to some paper to make a leaf print.

Or make a leaf rubbing. Turn a clean leaf face down, put a piece of paper over it, and rub gently with the side of a wax crayon.

Autumn experiments

Here are some experiments to do in the autumn.

Litter bugs

Bits of dead leaves and twigs are sometimes called leaf litter. Leaf litter makes a good autumn and winter shelter for insects and spiders.

Pick up a damp, dead leaf from the bottom of a pile. Look at it closely. Is there anything living on it? If you have a magnifying glass, you can have an even closer look.

Spider

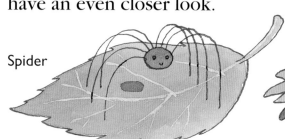

If the leaf is someone's home, put it back where you found it.

Wash your hands when you've finished your experiment.

Tiny jumping insects called springtails like leaf litter.

Centipedes crawl through soil and rotting leaves.

Measure the weather

Scientists measure the rain by collecting it in a **rain gauge**.

To make a rain gauge, you need some elastic bands, a ruler and a container with straight sides and a flat bottom.

Use the elastic bands to tie the ruler to the container, so that the measurements start at the bottom.

Leave the rain gauge outside in a safe place, like a yard or garden. You could put stones around it to make sure the wind doesn't blow it over.

Go back later to see how much rain has fallen. You could measure the rain at the same time every day, to see which is the wettest day of the week!

Words to remember

dew
Drops of water which collect on grass and plants overnight.

equator
The line around the middle of the Earth. There is no real line – it only appears on maps and globes.

evergreen
A tree, such as a pine tree, which does not lose its leaves in autumn.

festival
A party or feast to celebrate a special date.

calf
A baby cow. The plural of calf is calves.

collage
A picture made of things stuck on to paper.

combine harvester
A tractor that collects crops.

fog
A cloud of tiny water droplets close to the ground.

frost
Frozen water droplets that coat the ground, grass and trees in cold weather.

goddess
A female god.

Halloween
A celebration on 31 October when children dress up in costumes.

harvest
The time when farmers collect, or harvest, their crops.

Harvest Moon
The eighth full moon of the year, which comes during the harvest.

hibernate
To spend the winter asleep. Many animals hibernate.

Hindu
A member of the Hindu religion, which comes from India.

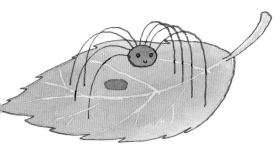

Indian summer
A few days of warm weather in the middle of autumn.

lantern
A kind of lamp.

marmot
A fat, furry burrowing animal about the size of a small dog.

migrate
To travel to another place for part of the year.

needles
Thin, dark green spikes which some trees have instead of leaves.

northern hemisphere
The northern half of the world, where Europe, America and Russia are.

North Pole
The most northern point on Earth.

pika
A small mountain animal that looks a bit like a mouse.

Pomona
A Roman autumn festival held to celebrate the harvest.

preserve
To make something last a long time.

pumpkin
A big, round, orange vegetable.

rain gauge
A container for measuring how much rain has fallen.

reflective
Reflective things make light bounce, or reflect, off them.

Romans
A powerful people who lived in Europe about 2000 years ago.

rose hip
A round fruit full of seeds that grows on rose bushes.

smog
A mixture of smoke and fog.

southern hemisphere
The southern half of the world, where Australia is.

South Pole
The most southern point on Earth.

tradition
Something people have done for a long time.

wither
To become old and dry.

Index